The Ultimate Language

with PLANTS AND FLOWERS O

including

Floral Emblems of the Scottish Clans

State Flowers of the U.S.A.

Chinese and Japanese Floral Calendars

and

Notes on the Care and Preparation

of Cut Flowers

by

Rob Cassy

To my mother and father

Rob Cassy, an authority on plant and flower lore, has
appeared on radio and television in Britain and Japan.
He lives and gardens in Greenwich.

**ABSON
BOOKS
LONDON**

5 Sidney Square London E1 2EY England
Telephone 020 7790 4737 Fax 020 7790 7346

First published in Great Britain January 2000
© Rob Cassy
Design and illustration by Alan Hughes
Printed in Malta
ISBN 0902920820

Introduction

A single, beautiful, red rose as a token of love might be the best known and most sought-after message in the language of flowers but, as this book reveals, it is merely the tip of the iceberg. Feelings and emotions we might hesitate to put into writing or be too shy or unsure of ourselves to speak out loud can be perfectly expressed instead with the simple gift of a well chosen single bloom or bunch of flowers.

You can offer someone your all with a spray of Shepherd's Purse picked from the wayside or you can proclaim the overwhelming happiness of your first emotions with an exquisite bouquet of Gardenia and Lilac. A feverish admirer sending Dittany could be encouraged with Carthamus or given the brush off with a dried white rose.

It is probably just as well that Dittany and Carthamus are none too easy to get hold of, but any good florist will be able to help you with most requirements. If you have a garden, or live in the country-side, many of the leaves and flowers in this book will be yours for the taking.

Steeped in history and tradition, the language of flowers has been with us since the recording of time. Featuring heavily in tales of the Greek and Roman Gods, flowers soon acquired a mythology of their own. So closely associated with the ebb and flow of the seasons, it was inevitable that certain flowers would become inextricably linked with the signs of the Zodiac.

The Bible is full of flower imagery, richest in The Song of Solomon. Floral allusions are so abundant in the works of Shakespeare that many have seeped into the national consciousness. Welsh Druids ascribed spiritual characteristics to trees and Scottish clansmen signified their allegiance with flower sprigs plucked from the glens. The Chinese and Japanese mark the passing months with floral calendars and every culture in the world has a rich store of practical and mystical plant lore.

In modern times every American State has proudly reinforced its regional identity by adopting a state flower. If flowers can be concrete symbols for abstract political boundaries, then even the least chivalrous among us can feel satisfied in using the language of flowers in affairs of the heart.

Rob Cassy.

How to use this Book

Whenever you receive a bunch of flowers, the first part of the book will help you detect any hidden meanings it contains. When you give flowers, the second part will help you choose those which best express your feelings. The final part of the book enables you to care for cut flowers and prolong their life.

Whether giving or receiving flowers, do not underestimate their conversational value. Everyone likes to feel special so, when giving flowers, why not tell the recipient their traditional meaning? When you receive a bouquet you can translate its symbolism with the aid of this book.

Contents

A to Z of Flowers	6	Official State Flowers of the USA	45
A to Z of Sentiments	21	Flowers of the Chinese Calendar	47
Plants and Flowers of the Zodiac	37	Flowers of the Japanese Calendar	47
Floral Emblems of the Scottish Clans	43	The Preparation and Care of Cut Flowers	48

THE LANGUAGE OF FLOWERS

A

Acacia	Platonic love
Acanthus	The Fine Arts. Artifice
Achillea	War
Aconite	Misanthropy
African Marigold	Vulgar minds
Agapanthus	Grace
Ageratum	Vivacious
Agrimony	Thankfulness. Gratitude
Alchemilla	Fashion
Allium	Health. Vitality
Allspice	Benevolence.Compassion
Almond Blossom	Hope. Indiscretion
Aloe	Grief. Acute sorrow
Alpinia	Desire. Passion
Alstroemeria	Innocence
Alyssum	Your worth exceeds even your beauty
Amaranthus	Immortality. Unfading love. Vanity
Amaryllis	Beauty. Pride. Haughtiness
Anemone	Anticipation. Transports of delight
Angelica	Inspiration
Anthurium	Boldness. Presumption
Apple	Temptation
Apple Blossom	Preference
Aquilegia	Modesty
Arbor-Vitae	Unchanging friendship
Arum Lily	Mourning. Purity. Ardour

Ash Tree	Grandeur
Aspen Tree	Lamentation
Asphodel	My regrets follow you to the grave
Aster	Variety. Daintiness
Astilbe	Reason
Astrantia	Hauteur
Auricula	Pride
Azalea	Abstinence. Temperance

B

Bachelor's Buttons	Celibacy. Hope in Love
Balm	Sympathy. Pleasantry
Balm of Gilead	Healing. Relief
Balsam	Impatience
Bamboo	Longevity

Banksia	Drama. Role playing.
Basil	Hatred
Bay Tree	Unchanging affection. Glory
Bear Grass	Utility
Beech Tree	Wealth
Begonia	Dark thoughts. Beware
Belladonna	Silence
Bells of Ireland	I will be with you in spirit
Betony	Surprise
Bilberry	Treachery
Birch Tree	Meekness
Bird of Paradise	Your love is my glory
Blackthorn	Adversity
Bluebell	Fidelity
Borage	Bluntness
Bouvardia	Sensuality

Box Tree	Stoicism
Bramble	Envy
Broom	Neatness. Humility
Bryony	Prosperity
Buddleia	Kisses
Bulrush	Docility
Bupleurum	Your love is returned
Buttercup	Prosperity. Ingratitude

C

Cabbage	Profit
Cactus	Warmth. I burn
Camellia	Loveliness. Excellence
Campanula	Gratitude
Campion	Youthful love
Candytuft	Indifference
Canna Lily	You rise above all others
Carnation	(Red, Pink or White) Pure love
Green Carnation	The love which dares not speak its name
Yellow Carnation	Scorn
Striped Carnation	Refusal
Carthamus	Do not hold back
Cedar Tree	Incorruptible
Celandine	Pleasure in store
Celosia	Vanity
Centaurea	Adoration
Chamomile	Relaxing the senses
Cherry Tree	Fortuitous. Education
Chestnut Tree	Do me justice
Chickweed	Rendezvous
Chicory	Meanness

Chincherinchee	A miracle. Annunciation
Chinese Lanterns	Lead me
Chrysanthemum	Cheerfulness
Cineraria	Glowing
Clematis	Beautiful mind
Clover	Be mine. Providence
Cloves	Dignity
Colchicum	My past is behind me
Coltsfoot	Justice shall be done
Columbine	Folly
Convolvulus	Bonds. Ties
Coriander	Hidden virtues
Corn	Wealth
Cornflower	Delicacy
Cowslip	Pensiveness. You are divine
Crocosmia	Bravery. Valour
Crocus	Cheerfulness. Joys of youth
Crown Imperial	Majesty. Power
Cyclamen	Resignation
Cypress Tree	Sadness. Mourning

D

Daffodil	Regretfulness. Regard
Dahlia	Instability
Daisy	Innocence
Dandelion	Oracle. Revealed wisdom
Daphne	Gilding the lily
Datura	Deceitful charms
Deadly Nightshade	Dark thoughts
Delphinium	Playfulness. Lack of commitment

Dittany	Burning lust
Dock	Solace. Healing
Dogwood	Durable love

E

Ebony	Morose. Depressed
Echinops	Sparring
Endive	Bitterness
Eglantine	Simplicity.
	I wound to heal
Elder	Zealousness.
	Magical powers
Elm	Dignity. Mourning
Eremurus	Attractive
Erigeron	Innocence
Eryngium	Sweetness in store

Eucharis Lily	Sentimental
Evening Primrose	Inconstancy

F

Fennel	Deserving praise.Strength
Fern	Sincerity. Fascination
Fig	Argument. Quarrelsome
Fig Tree	Prolific
Fir Tree	Lofty
Flax	Hard-working
Forget-Me-Not	True love
Foxglove	Insincerity
Freesia	Sweetness
French Marigold	Jealousy
Fritillary	Virtue under siege
Fuchsia	Good taste

Fumitory	Spitefulness

G

Gardenia	Overwhelming happiness
Gentian	You judge wrongly
Geranium	Comfort
Gerbera	Cheerfulness
Ginger	Desire. Passion
Gladiolus	Strong character
Gloriosa Lily	Glorious beauty
Gloxinia	Proud of spirit
Godetia	Your secret is safe with me
Goldenrod	Encouragement
Gooseberry	Anticipation
Gorse	Enduring affection
Grape Hyacinth	Playfulness
Grapes	Kindness. Charity
Grape Vine	Intoxication
Grass	Submission
Ground Ivy	Fidelity
Guelder Rose	Maturity. Experience
Gypsophila	Light-headed

H

Harebell	Grief
Hawthorn	Hope. Marriage
Hazel Tree	Reconciliation
Heartsease	You are in my thoughts
Heather	Solitude
Helenium	Tears
Helichrysum	I will value our love for ever

Heliconia	Exotic tastes
Heliotrope	Devotion
Hellebore	Fickleness
Hemlock	You will be the death of me
Henbane	Imperfection
Herb Robert	Piety
Hibiscus	Delicate beauty
Holly	Foresight
Hollyhock	Fruitfulness. Fecundity
Honesty	Honesty. Silence
Honeysuckle	Bonds of love
Hops	Injustice
Hornbeam Tree	Ornament
Horse Chestnut Tree	Luxury. Sensuality
Hoya	Classical beauty
Hyacinth	Teasing. Game-playing
Hydrangea	Heartless. Cold
Hypericum	Superstition
Hyssop	Purity. Fresh-faced honesty

I

Ice Plant	You are nothing to me. Disdain
Iris	A message. Hope
Ivy	Fidelity. Friendship. Ties
Ixia	I carry a torch for you

J

Jacob's Ladder	Come to me
Jasmine	Sensuality

Jonquil	Returned affection
Judas Tree	Betrayal
Juniper Tree	Protection

K

Kangaroo Paw	Tainted love
King Cups	Desire for riches

L

Laburnum	Forsaken
Larch Tree	Boldness
Larkspur	Levity. The lightness of your touch
Laurel	Glory
Lavender	Returned affection. Distrust

Lemon	Zest
Lemon Blossom	Fidelity
Leopard's Bane	Innocence
Liatris	Elegance
Lichen	Solitude
Lilac	First emotions. Memory
Lily	Purity. Virginity
Lily of the Valley	Returned happiness
Lime Tree	Conjugal love
Limonium	An intimate caress
Lobelia	Malevolence
London Pride	Frivolity
Lotus	Estranged love
Lupin	Dejection
Lychnis	Mysticism. Faith
Lysimachia	Archness

M

Magnolia	Magnificence. Dignity
Mahonia	You are everything to me
Mallow	Mildness
Maple Tree	Reserve
Marguerite	Optimistic
Marjoram	Shyness. Modesty
Meadowsweet	Usefulness
Mignonette	Hidden charms
Mimosa	Sensitivity
Mint	Virtue
Mistletoe	I surmount all obstacles
Mock Orange	Fraternal love
Monk's Hood	Chivalry
Morning Glory	Affection
Moss	Maternal love. Ennui
Mulberry Tree	Wisdom comes with age
Mushroom	Suspicion
Myrtle	Love. Fertility

N

Narcissus	Narcissism. Egotism
Nasturtium	Patriotism
Nemophila	Forgiveness
Nerine	Elegant. Detached
Nettle	Vexation. Cruelty. Spite
Nigella	Playfulness. Devilry

O

Oak Leaf	Bravery. Hospitality
Oak Tree	Longevity. A happy life ahead

Oats	To serenade. Consummation	*Pasque Flower*	Lack of pretension
		Passion Flower	Faith. Superstition
Oleander	Beware	*Peach Blossom*	Contentment. I am your captive
Olive Branch	Peace		
Onion	Domestic strife	*Pear Tree*	Riches and happiness
Orach	Solace	*Pelargonium*	Eagerness
Orange Blossom	Chastity. Wedding celebrations	*Pennyroyal*	Fly from me
		Penstemon	Unalloyed pleasure
Orchid	Beauty. Female sensuality	*Peony*	Shame. Bashfulness
Osier	Honesty. Frankness	*Peppers*	Agent provocateur
Osmunda	Dreams	*Periwinkle*	Memories of friendship
		Persicaria	Restoration
		Persimmon	Pleasured to excess
		Petunia	Do not despair
P		*Phlox*	Two hearts beating as one
Palm	Victory. A good omen	*Pimpernel*	An assignation
Pansy	Thoughts	*Pine Tree*	Pity. Dissolute
Parsley	Festivity. Entertainment		

Pink	Spirited affection
Plane Tree	Genius. Insight
Plums	Virility
Plum Tree	Fidelity
Polyanthus	Cupidity. Pride
Pomegranate	Good fortune. Success. Fecundity
Poplar Tree	Steadfastness
Poppy	Sleep. Dreaming. Reverie
Potato	Benevolence
Potentilla	I lay claim to your regard
Primrose	Youthfulness. Sadness
Privet	Abstinence. Prohibition
Protea	Protean. Flexible. Versatile

Q

Quaking Grass	Agitation
Queen Anne's Lace	Joy. Abundance
Quince	Temptation.

R

Ragged Robin	Wit
Ranunculus	Full of charm
Raspberry	Remorse. A stained past
Red Hot Poker	Amorous intent
Reeds	Music. Compliance
Rhododendron	Danger
Rhubarb	Advice
Rocket	Rivalry
Rose	Love
Red Rose	I love you

Red &White Roses	Partnership
White Rose	Innocence. Worthiness
Dried White Rose	Death is preferable to loss of innocence
Yellow Rose	Waning love
Variegated Rose	Caprice. Variety
Rose & Two buds	Secrecy
Dog Rose	Pleasure and pain
Rose Leaf	Hope. Anticipation
Rosemary	Remembrance
Rowan Tree	Charm
Rudbeckia	Justice
Rue	Disdain
Rye Grass	Vice

S

Saffron	Indulging to excess
Sage	Domestic virtue
Salvia	I think of you
Sandalwood	A keepsake
Scabious	Unfortunate attachment
Scilla	Forgive and forget
Scotch Thistle	Retaliation
Shamrock	Light-hearted. Affable
Shepherd's Purse	I offer you my all
Snapdragon	Presumption. No
Snowdrop	Hope
Soapwort	Delicacy always
Solidaster	Variety. Curiosity
Southernwood	Jest. Bantering
Speedwell	Semblance. Female fidelity

Stephanotis	Egotism
Stock	Lasting beauty
Stonecrop	Tranquillity
Straw	Union
A Broken Straw	A broken contract
Sumach	Splendour
Sunflower	Adoration. Haughtiness
Sweet Pea	Departure. Blissful rapture
Sweet William	Gallantry
Sycamore Tree	Curiosity

T

Tamarisk	Crime
Tansy	I declare war against you
Teasel	Misanthropy
Tendrils	Ties
Thistle	Austerity. Independence
Thorns	Severity
Thrift	Sympathy
Throatwort	Neglected beauty
Thyme	Activity. Valour
Traveller's Joy	Safety. Poverty
Trefoil	Unity. Revenge
Trillium	Modest beauty
Truffle	Surprise
Trumpet Flower	Flame. Separation
Tuberose	Dark pleasures. Voluptuousness

Red Tulip	Declaration of love
Yellow Tulip	Hopeless love
Variegated Tulip	Beautiful eyes
Tulip Tree	Fame
Turnip	Charity

U

Ulex	Domesticity
Umbrella Grass	Style. Sophistication
Urn Plant	A charming hostess

V

Valerian	Accommodating
Valotta	Beauty. Pride
Venus Fly Trap	Deceit

Red Verbena	Unite against evil
Pink Verbena	Family union
White Verbena	Spiritual union
Vernal Grass	Poor but happy
Veronica	Fidelity
Vervain	Enchantment
Violet	Faithfulness
White Violet	Candour
Yellow Violet	Rural happiness
Viper's Bugloss	Falsehood. Treachery
Virginia Creeper	I will cling to you always
Virgin's Bower	Filial love

W

Wallflower	Fidelity in adversity
Walnut	Intellect. Stratagem

Water Cress	Splendour
Water Lily	Pure of heart. Eloquent
Water Melon	Ampleness
Wax Flower	Susceptibility
Wheat	Riches
Willow Herb	Celibacy. Pretension.
Willow Tree	Mourning. Forsaken
Winter Cherry	Deception
Wisteria	Welcome. Clinging love
Witch Hazel	A spell. Spellbound
Wood Sorrel	Maternal tenderness
Wormwood	Absence

X

Xanthium	Rudeness. Pertinacity
Xeranthemum	Cheerfulness

Xerophyllum	Utility

Y

Yarrow	War
Yew Tree	Sorrow

Z

Zantedeschia	Mourning. Purity. Ardour
Zinnia	Absent friends

SENTIMENTS
and the flowers used to express them

A

Absence	Wormwood
Absent friends	Zinnia
Abstinence	Azalea. Privet
Abundance	Queen Anne's Lace
Accommodating	Valerian
Activity	Thyme
Acute sorrow	Aloe
Adoration	Centaurea
Adversity	Blackthorn
Advice	Rhubarb
Affable	Shamrock
Affection	Morning Glory
Agent provocateur	Peppers
Agitation	Quaking Grass
Amorous intent	Red Hot Poker
Ampleness	Water Melon
Annunciation	Chincherinchee
Anticipation	Anemone. Gooseberry. Rose Leaf
Archness	Lysimachia
Ardour	Arum Lily. Zantedeschia
Argument	Fig
Artifice	Acanthus
Assignation	Pimpernel
Attractive	Eremurus
Austerity	Thistle

21

B

Bantering	Southernwood
Bashfulness	Peony
Be mine	Clover
Beautiful eyes	Variegated tulip
Beautiful mind	Clematis
Beauty	Amaryllis. Orchid. Valotta
Benevolence	Allspice. Potato
Betrayal	Judas Tree
Beware	Begonia. Oleander
Bitterness	Endive
Bluntness	Borage
Boldness	Anthurium. Larch Tree
Bonds	Convolvulus
Bonds of love	Honeysuckle
Bravery	Crocosmia. Oak leaf
Burning lust	Dittany

C

Candour	White Violet
Caprice	Variegated Rose
Celibacy	Bachelor's Buttons.
	Willow Herb
Charity	Grapes. Turnip
Charm	Rowan Tree
Charming hostess	Urn Plant
Chastity	Orange Blossom
Cheerfulness	Chrysanthemum. Crocus.
	Gerbera. Xeranthemum
Chivalry	Monk's Hood
Classical beauty	Hoya
Clinging love	Wisteria
Cold	Hydrangea
Come to me	Jacob's Ladder

Comfort	Geranium
Compassion	Allspice
Compliance	Reeds
Conjugal love	Lime Tree
Consummation	Oats
Contentment	Peach Blossom
Crime	Tamarisk
Cruelty	Nettle
Cupidity	Polyanthus
Curiosity	Solidaster

D

Daintiness	Aster
Danger	Rhododendron
Dark pleasures	Tuberose
Dark thoughts	Begonia. Nightshade

Death is preferable to loss of innocence	Dried White Rose
Deceit	Venus Fly Trap
Deceitful charms	Datura
Deception	Winter Cherry
Declaration of love	Red Tulip
Dejection	Lupin
Delicacy	Cornflower. Soapwort
Delicate beauty	Hibiscus
Depressed	Ebony
Deserving Praise	Fennel
Desire	Alpinia. Ginger
Desire for riches	King Cups
Detached	Nerine
Devilry	Nigella
Devotion	Heliotrope
Dignity	Cloves. Elm. Magnolia

Disdain	Ice Plant. Rue.
Dissolute	Pine Tree
Distrust	Lavender
Do me justice	Chestnut Tree
Do not despair	Petunia
Do not hold back	Carthamus
Docility	Bulrush
Domestic strife	Onion
Domestic virtue	Sage
Domesticity	Ulex
Drama	Banksia
Dreaming	Poppy
Dreams	Osmunda
Durable love	Dogwood

E

Eagerness	Pelargonium
Education	Cherry Tree
Egotism	Narcissus. Stephanotis
Elegance	Liatris
Elegant	Nerine
Eloquent	Water Lily
Enchantment	Vervain
Encouragement	Goldenrod
Enduring affection	Gorse
Ennui	Moss
Entertainment	Parsley
Envy	Bramble
Estranged love	Lotus
Excellence	Camellia
Exotic tastes	Heliconia
Experience	Guelder Rose

F

Faith	Lychnis. Passion Flower
Faithfulness	Violet
Falsehood	Viper's Bugloss
Fame	Tulip Tree
Family union	Pink Verbena
Fascination	Fern
Fashion	Alchemilla
Fecundity	Hollyhock. Pomegranate
Fickleness	Hellebore
Female fidelity	Speedwell
Female sensuality	Orchid
Fertility	Myrtle
Festivity	Parsley
Fidelity	Bluebell. Ground Ivy. Plum Tree. Veronica. Lemon Blossom
Fidelity in adversity	Wallflower
Filial love	Virgin's Bower
Fine arts	Acanthus
First emotions	Lilac
Flame	Trumpet Flower
Flexible	Protea
Fly from me	Pennyroyal
Folly	Columbine
Forgive and forget	Scilla
Forgiveness	Nemophila
Forsaken	Laburnum. Willow Tree
Foresight	Holly
Fortuitous	Cherry Tree
Frankness	Osier
Fraternal love	Mock Orange
Fresh-faced honesty	Hyssop
Friendship	Ivy

Frivolity	London Pride
Fruitfulness	Hollyhock
Full of charm	Ranunculus

G

Game-playing	Hyacinth
Genius	Plane Tree
Gilding the lily	Daphne
Glorious beauty	Gloriosa Lily
Glory	Bay Tree. Laurel
Glowing	Cineraria
Good fortune	Pomegranate
Good omen	Palm
Good taste	Fuchsia
Grace	Agapanthus
Grandeur	Ash Tree

Gratitude	Agrimony. Campanula
Grief	Aloe. Harebell

H

Happiness	Gardenia
Hard-working	Flax
Hatred	Basil
Haughtiness	Amaryllis. Astrantia.
Healing	Balm of Gilead. Dock
Health	Allium
Heartless	Hydrangea
Hidden charms	Mignonette
Hidden virtues	Coriander
Honesty	Honesty. Osier
Hope	Almond Blossom. Hawthorn. Iris. Rose Leaf. Snowdrop

Hope in love	Bachelor's Buttons
Hopeless love	Yellow Tulip
Hospitality	Oak Leaf
Humility	Broom

I

I burn	Cactus
I carry a torch for you	Ixia
I declare war against you	Tansy
I lay claim to your regard	Potentilla
I love you	Red Rose
I offer you my all	Shepherd's Purse
I surmount all obstacles	Mistletoe
I think of you	Salvia
I will be with you in spirit	Bells of Ireland
I will cling to you always	Virginia Creeper
I will value our love forever	Helichrysum
I wound to heal	Eglantine
Immortality	Amaranthus
Impatience	Balsam
Imperfection	Henbane
Inconstancy	Evening Primrose
Incorruptible	Cedar Tree
Independence	Thistle
Indifference	Candytuft

Indiscretion	Almond Blossom
Indulging to excess	Saffron
Ingratitude	Buttercup
Injustice	Hops
Innocence	Alstroemeria. Daisy. Erigeron. Leopard's Bane. White Rose
Insight	Plane Tree
Insincerity	Foxglove
Inspiration	Angelica
Instability	Dahlia
Intellect	Walnut
Intimate caress	Limonium
Intoxication	Grape Vine

J

Jealousy	French Marigold
Jest	Southernwood
Joy	Queen Anne's Lace
Joys of youth	Crocus
Justice	Rudbeckia
Justice shall be done	Coltsfoot

K

Keepsake	Sandalwood
Kindness	Grapes
Kisses	Buddleia

L

Lack of commitment	Delphinium
Lack of pretension	Pasque Flower
Lamentation	Aspen Tree
Lasting beauty	Stock
Lead me	Chinese Lanterns
Levity	Larkspur
Light-headed	Gypsophila
Light-hearted	Shamrock
The lightness of your touch	Larkspur
Lofty	Fir Tree
Longevity	Bamboo. Oak Tree
Love	Myrtle. Rose
The love which dares not speak its name	Green Carnation
Loveliness	Camellia
Luxury	Horse Chestnut Tree

M

Magical powers	Elder
Magnificence	Magnolia
Majesty	Crown Imperial
Malevolence	Lobelia
Marriage	Hawthorn
Maternal love	Moss
Maternal tenderness	Wood Sorrel
Maturity	Guelder Rose
Meanness	Chicory

Meekness	Birch Tree
Memories of friendship	Periwinkle
Memory	Lilac
Message	Iris
Mildness	Mallow
Miracle	Chincherinchee
Misanthropy	Aconite. Teasel
Modest beauty	Trillium
Modesty	Aquilegia. Marjoram
Morose	Ebony
Mourning	Arum Lily.Zantedeschia Cypress. Elm. Willow
Music	Reeds
My past is behind me	Colchicum
My regrets follow you to the grave	Asphodel

Mysticism	Lychnis

N

Narcissism	Narcissus
Neatness	Broom
Neglected beauty	Throatwort
No	Snapdragon

O

Optimistic	Marguerite
Oracle	Dandelion
Ornament	Hornbeam Tree
Overwhelming happiness	Gardenia

P

Passion	Passion Alpinia. Ginger
Patriotism	Nasturtium
Peace	Olive Branch
Pensiveness	Cowslip
Pertinacity	Xanthium
Piety	Herb Robert
Pity	Pine Tree
Platonic love	Acacia
Playfulness	Delphinium. Grape Hyacinth. Nigella
Pleasantry	Balm
Pleasure and pain	Dog Rose
Pleasure in store	Celandine
Pleasured to excess	Persimmon
Poor but happy	Vernal Grass
Poverty	Traveller's Joy
Power	Crown Imperial
Praise	Fennel
Preference	Apple Blossom
Presumption	Anthurium. Snapdragon
Pretension	Willow Herb
Pride	Amaryllis. Auricula. Polyanthus. Valotta
Profit	Cabbage
Prohibition	Privet
Prolific	Fig Tree
Prosperity	Bryony. Buttercup
Protean	Protea
Protection	Juniper Tree
Proud of spirit	Gloxinia
Providence	Clover
Pure love	Carnation
Pure of heart	Water Lily

Purity	Arum Lily Zantedeschia. Hyssop. Lily	*Rendezvous*	Chickweed
		Reserve	Maple Tree
		Resignation	Cyclamen
Q		*Restoration*	Persicaria
		Retaliation	Scotch Thistle
Quarrelsome	Fig	*Returned affection*	Jonquil
		Return of happiness	Lily of the Valley
		Returned affection	Lavender
R		*Revealed wisdom*	Dandelion
Reason	Astilbe	*Revenge*	Trefoil
Reconciliation	Hazel Tree	*Reverie*	Poppy
Refusal	Striped Carnation	*Riches*	Wheat
Regard	Daffodil	*Riches*	Pear Tree
Regretfulness	Daffodil	*Rivalry*	Rocket
Relaxing the senses	Chamomile	*Role playing*	Banksia
Relief	Balm of Gilead	*Rudeness*	Xanthium
Remembrance	Rosemary	*Rural happiness*	Yellow Violet
Remorse	Raspberry		

S

Sadness	Cypress Tree. Primrose
Safety	Traveller's Joy
Scorn	Yellow Carnation
Secrecy	Rose & Two Buds
Semblance	Speedwell
Sensitivity	Mimosa
Sensuality	Bouvardia. Horse Chestnut Tree. Jasmine
Sentimental	Eucharis Lily
Separation	Trumpet Flower
Serenade	Oats
Severity	Thorns
Shame	Peony
Shyness	Marjoram
Silence	Belladonna. Honesty
Simplicity	Eglantine
Sincerity	Fern
Sleep	Poppy
Solace	Dock. Orach
Solitude	Heather. Lichen
Sophistication	Umbrella Grass
Sorrow	Aloe. Yew Tree
Sparring	Echinops
Spellbound	Witch Hazel
Splendour	Water Cress
Spirited affection	Pink
Spiritual union	White Verbena
Spite	Nettle. Fumitory
Stained past	Raspberry
Steadfastness	Poplar Tree
Stoicism	Box Tree
Stratagem	Walnut
Strength	Fennel

Strong character	Gladiolus
Style	Umbrella Grass
Submission	Grass
Success	Pomegranate
Superstition	Passion Flower. Hypericum
Surprise	Betony. Truffle
Susceptibility	Wax Flower
Suspicion	Mushroom
Sweetness	Freesia
Sweetness in store	Eryngium
Sympathy	Balm. Thrift

T

Tainted love	Kangaroo Paw
Tears	Helenium

Teasing	Hyacinth
Temperance	Azalea
Temptation	Apple. Quince
Thankfulness	Agrimony
Thoughts	Pansy
Ties	Ivy. Convolvulus. The Tendrils of any Climber
Tranquillity	Stonecrop
Transports of delight	Anemone
Treachery	Bilberry. Viper's Bugloss
True love	Forget-Me-Not
Two hearts beating as one	Phlox

U

Unalloyed pleasure Penstemon
Unchanging affection Bay Tree
Unchanging friendship Arbor-Vitae
Unfading love Amaranthus
Unfortunate attachment Scabious
Unite against evil Red Verbena
Usefulness Meadowsweet
Utility Bear Grass. Xerophyllum

V

Valour Crocosmia. Thyme
Vanity Amaranthus. Celosia
Variety Aster. Solidaster. Variegated Rose
Versatile Protea
Vexation Nettle
Vice Rye Grass
Victory Palm
Virginity Lily
Virility Plums
Virtue Mint
Virtue under siege Fritillary
Vitality Allium
Vivacious Ageratum
Voluptuousness Tuberose
Vulgar minds African Marigold

W

Waning love Yellow Rose
War Achillea. Tansy. Yarrow

Warmth	Cactus
Wealth	Beech Tree. Corn
Wedding	
celebrations	Orange Blossom
Welcome	Wisteria
Wisdom comes	
with age	Mulberry Tree
Wit	Ragged Robin
Worthiness	White Rose

You are nothing to me	IcePlant
You judge wrongly	Gentian
You rise above all others	Canna Lily
You will be the death of me	Hemlock
Your love is my glory	Bird of Paradise
Your love is returned	Bupleurum
Your secret is safe with me	Godetia
Your worth exceeds even	
your beauty	Alyssum
Youthful love	Campion
Youthfulness	Primrose

X

Y

You are divine	Cowslip
You are everything to me	Mahonia
You are in my thoughts	Heartsease

Z

Zealousness	Elder
Zest	Lemon

PLANTS and FLOWERS of the ZODIAC

ARIES 21st March - 19th April ♈
The Ram

TAURUS 20th April - 20th May ♉
The Bull

Fire and Iron are the elemental qualities of assertive Ariens, who are ruled by the war-like planet Mars

Earth and copper are the characteristic elements of sensual and practical Taureans. They are ruled by Venus, planet of love

Birthstones	Diamond, Ruby
Colours	Black, Red, White
Flowers	Amaranthus, Carnation, Heliconia, Hippeastrum, Rose, Tansy

Birthstone	Topaz
Colours	Green, Pastels
Flowers	Aquilegia, Bells of Ireland, Forget-Me-Not, Grape Hyacinth, Lilac Mallow

GEMINI 21st May - 20th June Ⅱ
The Twins

Air and Quicksilver are the elements influencing capricious, intuitive Geminians, whose ruling planet is Mercury

Birthstones	Garnet, Tourmaline
Colours	Orange, Pale Blue, White
Flowers	Orange Blossom, Orchid, Scilla, Sweet Pea, Tiger Lily, Tuberose

CANCER 21st June - 22nd July ♋
The Crab

Water and Silver are the elements behind the shrewdness and compassion of typical Cancerians. Their changing moods are influenced by the waxing and waning of the Moon

Birthstones	Amber, Moonstone, Pearl
Colours	Indigo, Orange, Yellow
Flowers	Freesia, Honesty, Lotus, Marguerite, Scabious, Stephanotis

LEO 23rd July - 22nd August ♌
The Lion

The elemental qualities of Fire and Gold inform the proud and courageous Leonine temperament. Leos are ruled by the Sun

Birthstones	Chrysolite, Tiger Eye
Colours	Orange, Yellow
Flowers	Crocosmia, Laurel, Marigold, Palm, Sunflower, Valotta

VIRGO 23rd August - 22nd September ♍
The Virgin

Earth and Quicksilver are the characteristic elements of gentle and demonstrative Virgoans. They are ruled by the planet Mercury, and by the mythological Vulcan, god of thunder

Birthstones	Agate, Opal, Peridot
Colours	Brown, Eau de Nil, White
Flowers	Astrantia, Euphorbia, Lavender, Lily, Lupin, Vervain

LIBRA 23rd September - 22nd October
♎ The Scales

Air and Copper are the elements helping practical Librans put their plans into action. Always charming, they are ruled by the planet Venus

Birthstones	Emerald
Colours	Green, Pink, Purple
Flowers	Aloe, Hydrangea, Iris, Myrtle, Rose, Veronica

SCORPIO 23rd October - 21st November
♏ The Scorpion

Harnessing the elements Water and Iron, the Scorpionic succeed as much by stealth as by direct action. Their ruling planets are Mars and Pluto

Birthstones	Ruby, Turquoise
Colours	Crimson, Blue-green
Flowers	Aconite, Cactus, Chrysanthemum, Nettle, Poppy, Red Hot Poker

SAGITTARIUS 22nd November - 21st December ♐ The Archer

Idealistic and sensual Sagittarians have the elemental qualities of Fire and Tin. They are ruled by the planet Jupiter

Birthstone	Lapis Lazuli
Colours	Blue, Purple, White
Flowers	Centaurea, Echinops,
Fig,	Hyssop, Oak,
	Sweet William

CAPRICORN 22nd December - 19th January ♑ The Goat

Earth and Lead are the characteristic elements of resourceful and sure-footed Capricorneans. They are ruled by Saturn, planet of fate and wisdom

Birthstones	Diamond, Jet, Onyx,
	Ruby
Colours	Black, Green, Violet
Flowers	Acanthus, Delphinium,
	Gladiolus, Mint, Willow,
	Zantedeschia

AQUARIUS 20th January - 18th February
♒ The Watercarrier

The elements of loyal yet free-thinking Aquarians are Air and Lead. They are ruled jointly by Saturn and Uranus

Birthstones	Garnet, Sapphire, Topaz
Colours	Turquoise, Yellow
Flowers	Agapanthus, Anemone, Gardenia, Tulip, Mahonia, Urn Plant

PISCES 19th February - 20th March ♓
The Fish

Shy, creative and mystical Pisceans have the elemental qualities of Water and Tin. They are ruled on the one hand by expansive Jupiter, on the other by Neptune - planet of dreams and unreality

Birthstones	Amethyst, Bloodstone, Pearl
Colours	Blue, Green, Violet
Flowers	Hyacinth, Lily, Narcissus, Opium Poppy, Violet, All water plants

FLORAL EMBLEMS of the SCOTTISH CLANS

Buchanan	Birch, Blaeberry
Cameron	Bearberry, Oak
Campbell	Bog myrtle, Club moss
Chisholm	Alder, Fern
Colquhoun	Bearberry, Dogberry, Hazel
Cumming	Sallow
Davidson	Box, Red Whortleberry
Dewar	Birch, Blaeberry
Drummond	Holly, Wild Thyme
Duncan	Heather, Bracken
Farquharson	Box, Foxglove, Red Whortleberry
Ferguson	Poplar, Rock Rose, Sundew
Forbes	Broom
Fraser	Yew, Strawberry Leaf
Gordon	Ivy
Graham	Spurge Laurel
Grant	Cranberry, Pine
Gunn	Rosewort, Juniper
Hay	Mistletoe
Lamont	Crab Apple Tree, Heather
Logan	Whin
McAllister	Heather
McAulay	Cranberry, Pine
Macdonald	Heather
Macdonell	Heather
Macdougall	Cypress, Heather, Pine
Macduff	Box, Red Whortleberry
Macfarlane	Cloudberry, Cranberry, Heather
Macgregor	Pine

Macintosh	Box, Red Whortleberry	**Menzies**	Ash, Heather
Mackay	Broom, Bulrush	**Munro**	Club Moss
Mackenzie	Deer Grass, Holly	**Murray**	Butcher's Broom, Juniper
Mackinnon	Pine, St. John's Wort	**Ogilvie**	Hawthorn
Maclauchlan	Heather, Mountain Ash, Periwinkle	**Oliphant**	Bulrush, Maple
		Robertson	Bracken, Heather
Maclean	Bearberry, Holly	**Rose**	Briar, Wild Rosemary
Macleod	Juniper, Red Whortleberry	**Ross**	Bearberry, Juniper
		Sinclair	Broom, Clover, Whin
Macmillan	Deer Grass	**Stewart**	Oak, Thistle, White Rose
Macneil	Heather	**Sutherland**	Bulrush, Broom, Butcher's Broom
Macnab	Cloudberry, Pine		
Macnaughtan	Heather, Mountain Azalea	**Urquhart**	Wallflower
Macpherson	Box, Heather, Red Whortleberry		
Macquarrie	Pine		
Macrae	Club Moss		

OFFICIAL STATE FLOWERS of the U.S.A.

Alabama	Goldenrod
Alaska	Forget-Me-Not
Arizona	Saguaro (Giant Cactus)
Arkansas	Apple Blossom
California	Californian Poppy
Colorado	Blue Columbine
Connecticut	Mountain Laurel
Delaware	Peach Blossom
Florida	Orange Blossom
Georgia	Cherokee Rose
Hawaii	Hibiscus
Idaho	Mock Orange
Illinois	Native Violet
Indiana	Zinnia, Peony
Iowa	Wild Rose
Kansas	Sunflower
Kentucky	Goldenrod
Louisiana	Magnolia Grandiflora
Maine	Pine Cone
Maryland	Black-eyed Susan
Massachusetts	Trailing Arbutus
Michigan	Apple Blossom
Minnesota	Showy Lady's Slipper
Mississippi	Magnolia Grandiflora
Missouri	Downy Hawthorn
Montana	Bitter Root
Nebraska	Goldenrod
Nevada	Sagebrush
New Hampshire	Purple Lilac

New Jersey	Native Violet	Vermont	Red Clover
New Mexico	Yucca	Virginia	Flowering Dogwood
New York	Rose	Washington	Coast Rhododendron
North Carolina	Flowering Dogwood	West Virginia	Great Rhododendron
North Dakota	Prairie Rose	Wisconsin	Native Violet
Ohio	Scarlet Carnation	Wyoming	Indian Paintbrush
Oklahoma	Mistletoe	District of	
Oregon	Oregon Hilly Grape (Mahonia)	Columbia	American Beauty Rose
Pennsylvania	Mountain Laurel		
Rhode Island	Native Violet		
South Carolina	Yellow Jessamine		
South Dakota	American Pasque Flower		
Tennessee	Iris		
Texas	Texas Bluebonnet		
Utah	Sego Lily		

Green Lane.

Public house closures are nothing new – the King's Arms and Rising Sun at Churchstanton were de-licensed in the 20th century.

Brimley Hill view.

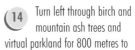 **(12)** Pass Wildwood House and Applehayes Cottage in 700 metres. Turn right (E) through the next field gate, opposite a green lane, and descend across the pasture to a stile and rushy track through the trees. Cross a track. Proceed to the lakes in 300 metres and pass between them. Bear right and then left, in 100 metres, on the grassy slope. Head uphill, following the bank beside Ringdown Nature Reserve for 400 metres to Downlands Lane.

(13) Turn right, down and around the corner, to the gate on the following bend in 200 metres.

(14) Turn left through birch and mountain ash trees and virtual parkland for 800 metres to

Burnworthy Farm. Turn right into laurel bushes and mixed woodland in 100 metres.

(15) Turn right (S) for 200 metres. Then follow the woodland fence across stiles and through holly bushes to the left of Venn Farm in 400 metres. Continue up its drive, which crosses a stream, to the corner in 150

metres. Enter the left-hand of the two fields facing you. Keep the hedgerow to your right and continue straight ahead at the stile with rushy scrub to the right.

(16) Join the road at Newtons in 300 metres and turn right, uphill, to a de-licensed public house on the corner in 200 metres. Turn left to return to the parish church in 100 metres.

Churchstanton bier and stocks.

Final parking place.

Negotiating a stile.

5 Castle Neroche and Blackwater

A short forest walk around the mediaeval fortress of the northern escarpment

Overlooking Taunton Deane from a precipitous escarpment, Castle Neroche was the stronghold of the Blackdown Hills in the early Middle Ages. Since covered in trees, and declared as access land by the Forestry Commission, it is the delightful hub for a network of woodland walks, seen at their best in bluebell time. Floristically, there is always something to enjoy — from verge-side cowslips to masses of hedgerow foxgloves. The woods have their deer and amphibians, and even the occasional snake, though they should hear you coming. Alpacas are the new-age livestock in adjoining pastures.

Level: ♥ ♥
Length: 4 miles
Terrain: Easy paths which would be a doddle but for the inevitable steep slope.
Park & start: In the car-park provided by the Forestry Commission beside Castle Neroche, which is reached by turning north from the A303 at the Eagle Tavern, towards Wellington, and taking the fourth turning on the east side.
Start ref: ST 274 156
Postcode: TA20 3LB
Websites:
www.forestry.gov.uk
www.nerochescheme.org

① Set off into the earthworks (NW) and climb steps to the Castle Keep, after the big ditch beyond the inner bailey – now a farmyard – in 300 metres. Turn left at the top and do a circuit of the main mound to return to the gate into Castle Neroche Farm in 150 metres. Go through the farmyard and follow the drive (SW) down to the road in 500 metres.

② Turn left and immediately right, into a cul-de-sac lane, for 150 metres. Turn right, through the hedge, and then left to pass to the right of the house. Bear left in the next pasture, following the hedgerow down to the stream. Walk uphill between the alpaca paddock and the arable field to the road in Blackwater hamlet in 400 metres.

Castle Neroche summit.

Ascending the motte.

3 Turn right (W), up the lane, and continue straight ahead at the first junction beside Penny's Cottage to the main road in 350 metres.

4 Cross to the bridleway into the trees. Follow it (NW) down to the forest road across former Staple Common in 300 metres.

Robert, Count of Mortain seems to have been the builder of the Norman Conquest fortress of Castle Neroche, apparently on the lesser earthworks of an Iron Age hill-fort, with banks and ditches across the spur to defend a palisaded ringwork.

Castle Keep.

Western slopes.

5 Turn right (E) along, around and then down to the main road in 1,000 metres.

6 Cross to the track on the other side. Follow the woodland ride around to the left (NE) in 150 metres. Continue for 500 metres to a cluster of multiple path junctions with two options on each side.

The huge motte or keep at Castle Neroche was added in the 12th century for a high timber tower that would have been visible from Taunton.

Neroche forest.

Cowslip time.

(7) Take the first on the left (N), down a bridleway which becomes rushy Green Lane and emerges beside fields above Lane End Farm in 600 metres.

(8) Turn right at the main road, for just 50 metres, and then right (SE) into a lane. Curland Church is across to the left. Continue straight on uphill from the corner, in 400 metres, beside Mount Pleasant. After Annadale and Alfords, in 350 metres, the surfaced track then continues straight ahead up into the wood.

Castle Neroche Farm.

A wayside stone at Blackwater is to 92-year-old Samuel Hallett who died in 1869 after having built a chapel and 'preached the gospel here over 40 years'.

Hedgerow foxgloves.

9 On the other side of the wood, in 500 metres, we approach fields and the view across Castle Farm. Turn abruptly right (SW) for the ascent of the escarpment.

10 Bear left in 200 metres to continue up the main slope. Re-enter the earthworks in a further 350 metres and turn left (S) in 50 metres, to the car-park, in a further 50 metres.

Top:
Mount Pleasant.

Bottom:
Blackwater.

6 **Otterford and Birchwood**

A short walk around Otterford, its nearby hamlet and 'lost park' lakeland

Otterhead Lakes with 233 acres of parkland and pastures are owned by Wessex Water. They cover the catchment below the source of the Otter, in order to control the quality and flow of potable water, abstracted further down the river system. Royston Water woodland is managed by the Forestry Commission its string of lakes and ponds by Somerset Wildlife Trust. They were landscaped for an imposing country mansion – Otterhead House – which has since been demolished. Otterford village is now no more than its parish church and Church Farm. The main hamlet, with its own mission church in an incredibly picturesque setting, is over the barrow-studded hill in Birchwood.

Otterford.

Level: 🐾

Length: 4.5 miles

Terrain: Reasonable to good for the Blackdown Hills without serious slopes.

Park & start: From the lay-by opposite St Leonard's Church at Otterford

Start ref: ST 222 142

Postcode: TA3 7EE

Public transport: None

Websites:
www.somersetwildlife.org.uk
www.wessexwater.com

Fyfett monkey puzzle.

1 Set off along the lane (E), away from the farm, to the corner in 50 metres. Proceed straight ahead into a stub-end of green lane, to a gate and stile, and follow the hedgerow. Keep it to your right and then cross the pasture beside School Farm in 700 metres. Tree-covered Robin Hood's Butts are to the right.

2 Cross at the junction, down the lane beside Fernleigh, and Fyfett Farm with its 100-feet tall monkey puzzle. Continue to the corner and stream, in the valley floor, in 600 metres.

3 Turn right (NE), through the gate, up the slope to the top corner of the pasture in 150 metres. Follow the hedgerow straight ahead for 200 metres. Pass the first gate after the oak tree and also the cattle-trough but then turn immediately right (SE) through the second gate. The track beside the hedgerow becomes a green lane.

4 Turn right (SW) on reaching a concrete road in 250 metres, down into Owlhayes Farm, in 50 metres. Turn left (SE) into the field beside and below the farmhouse. The track beside the hedge leads down to

As tall as those in their native Chilean forests, the magnificent monkey puzzle tree on the front lawn of Fyfett Farm was planted in 1861 when the house – dating from 1677 – was restored.

Church Farm.

the valley bottom in 200 metres. Bear right on the other side, across the stream and up the slope, and pass to the left of Anglican Birchwood Chapel-of-ease in the clearing, in 300 metres. Proceed to the road in 200 metres.

5 Turn right (SW), downhill from the Old Forge, and proceed straight ahead from the junction in 100 metres. Pass Birchwood Cottage, Birchwood House, Sunny Side and

Owlshayes stream.

Bray Cottage, in their series of idyllic settings. Cross the stream in 250 metres and continue uphill to Waterhayes Farm in 200 metres.

6 Turn left (SE) after the thatched house, opposite the gate to Waterhayes Cottage and continue straight ahead through the central gate into the fields and keep the hedge to your left for 150 metres. Continue straight ahead

The line of prehistoric burial mounds known as Robin Hood's Butts, plus three big mounds in fields beyond, date from between 2100 and 1500 BC and comprise the principal Bronze Age cemetery on the Blackdown Hills.

across the arable field to the gate and trees in 200 metres. Bear left to pass below Rull Farm, via a gate in the hedge, and join the road in 200 metres.

7 Turn right (SW), uphill, and cross the main road (W) in 700 metres. Another two of Robin Hood Butts — prehistoric burial mounds — are across to the left. Bear left (SW) at the junction in 500 metres. Continue down to Royston Water and the junction beside Webbers Farmhouse in 600 metres.

Birchwood Chapel.

Chapel gates.

Thought to have been a stopping point for pilgrims between Exeter and Glastonbury, mediaeval St Leonard's Church at Otterford was expanded in 1861 to cater for staff on the newly-created Otterhead Estate.

Sunny Side.

(8) Turn right (W) to cross the River Otter over Royston Bridge. Turn right (N) into a soggy green lane in 100 metres. Turn right in 150 metres, to leave the public path for a permissive path through Otterhead Lakes nature reserve. This follows the bank of the long lake, and passes ponds beyond, to rejoin the public path network beside the dam of the second lake in 750 metres.

(9) Turn right, away from the house, uphill through laurels and rhododendrons to the car-park in 300 metres.

(10) Turn left at the road, round the corner beside Otterhead Lodge to return to St Leonard's Church in 300 metres.

William Beadon (died 1864) turned ancient Week Farm into Otterhead House – 'one of the handsomest seats in the neighbourhood' – and was succeeded by High Court judge Sir John Mellor (died 1887).

Otterhead upper lake.

7 Smeatharpe and Bolham Water

A 6-mile circuit through a squelchy summertime landscape in the heart of the hills

Level: ♥ ♥
Length: 6 miles
Terrain: Squelchy conditions are to be expected for most of the year but there are no long-haul climbs.
Park and start: At the western end of Smeatharpe hamlet or nearby in the vicinity of the disused airfield or Newhouse Baptist Church.
Start ref: ST 197 102
Postcode: EX14 9RF
Public transport: Buses from Honiton to Taunton.
Websites:
www.devon.gov.uk
www.wikipedia.org.uk/raf-upottery

Something about Smeatharpe may seem familiar. Helped by the presence of a 40-mm Bofors anti-aircraft gun, plus masses of concrete runways still in situ, Smeatharpe Aerodrome remains a wartime time-warp. Where you may have seen it before, on television, was as the backdrop to the *'Band of Brothers'* mini-series in 2001. Below, in contrast, an acid heathland site of special scientific interest drops away across Gotleigh Moor and Southey Moor with a remarkable range of primitive bog plants, including insect-eating sundews, and both ground and woodland fungi. Expect to see buzzards and ravens, and to hear exotic calls from a captive collection of birds, at Bolham Brook.

Baker's Farm
Cleve Farm
8
9
10
Rainbow Crest
11
7
Hart's Farm
Bolham River
am
er
Middleton Barton
Bolham Brook
12
Burcombe Farm
6
SOUTHAY MOOR
4
3
Springdale
5
13
Valentine's Farm
scale 500m
N
2
GOTLEIGH MOOR
1
Bloomers Farm
+ Newhouse Baptist Church

Smeatharpe runway.

Bofors gun.

Buildings dispersed around Smeatharpe Aerodrome included seven clusters of Nissen huts which accommodated a total of 2,500 air and ground crew, ancillary staff and troops in transit.

(1) Set off from the Smeatharpe Aerodrome side of Bloomers Farm, on the opposite side of the road, through the gate between Vivery House and Ash Cottage. Follow the bridleway (NW) across the field, diagonally, to the right-hand of the two gates in 200 metres. Keep former Smeatharpe Aerodrome and its surviving buildings to your left.

(2) Continue through the following gates as well, into the hillside grassland of Gotleigh Moor. Keep the wartime airfield and its surviving buildings up to the left. Go through a gate beside the upper boundary, in 200 metres, and continue straight ahead across the next section of access land for 200 metres. Cross the stream and go through a gate in

another 200 metres. Now follow the upper hedgerow beside a ruined cowshed, into a green lane up to the pasture beside Valentine's Farm in 400 metres.

3 Pass to the right of the first buildings and then turn left through the gate. Continue straight ahead in 25 metres, up the drive, following the bridleway sign. Take the right-hand of the two gates beside a pond in 200 metres. Continue to follow the drive, around a pasture and down to a tarred road in 300 metres.

4 Turn left (W), through Middleton Barton, to a road junction in 300 metres.

Newhouse Baptist Church – built in 1859 – replaced the Particular and Calvanistic Chapel dating from the time of the Five Mile Act in 1652 which was located here for easy escape from Devon into adjacent parts of Somerset and Dorset.

Newhouse Chapel.

Dakota transports carrying paratroops of the United States 101st Airborne Division took off for D-Day, from RAF Upottery – Smeatharpe Aerodrome – in the early hours of 6 June 1944.

5 Turn right (N) for 50 metres and then left (W) through a field gate. Follow the track beside the hedgerow straight ahead to the end of the long hillside pasture in 750 metres. Enter the beech trees of Middleton Wood and follow the path around to the right (NW), down an incline terrace to the left-hand of two field gates in 250 metres. Continue downhill, into the pasture, towards Burcombe Farm. Keep to the left of a bog and cross the stream at a footbridge in 300 metres.

6 Turn right, below the farm, and follow the stream into the next pasture in 150 metres. Bear left to a gate beside the road in 125 metres. Turn right, up the drive and away from the farm, to the road junction in 150 metres. Turn right, downhill across the bridge, and up into Bolham Water hamlet in 200 metres.

7 Turn right (NE) just after the turning to Bolham Mill, uphill to Meadowhayes and Hart's Farm in 300 metres. Join a green lane up the steeper hillside beyond. Follow the hedge for the final ascent to a gate on to the road at the top in 300 metres.

Bolham Water.

Sculptural decay.

8 Turn right (E) and then continue straight ahead at the junction, along the hilltop lane above Lytchett Farm. Follow the road around a bend in 600 metres and down to the next corner in 150 metres.

9 Turn left and follow the hedgerow track to Baker's Farm, after three pastures, in 600 metres. Go through the outer farmyard and turn right to the gate in 25 metres — after the stone barn.

10 Continue straight ahead across the hilltop pasture to a hunting gate beneath the trees in 150 metres and then follow the hedgerow at the head of the valley. Head for the tall beech tree at the top of the slope in 350 metres. Cross the stiles. Pass to the right of Clivehayes Farm and then Cleve Farm in 250 metres.

11 Turn right (S) along the road, towards the valley, and pass the bungalow in 150 metres. Turn right

(SW) through the field gate after the entrance to Rainbow Crest. Bear left, down to the big beech trees, in 200 metres. Cross the stile to the left of them. Bear right down to a stile in the lower fence in 100 metres. Enter the wood and walk down (S) a squelchy and stony double-banked lane. This passes to the right of a little lakeland and aviaries at Bolham Brook in 200 metres. Turn right along the drive to the road in 50 metres.

Southey Moor.

Bracket fungi.

12 Turn left (SE), uphill for 150 metres, and then right along a bridleway. Follow the hedgerow and then a boggy track straight ahead across marshy and scrubby Southey Moor for 1,000 metres. Go through the gates into the second section of this site of special scientific interest. It had off-putting notices when we researched the walk. Exercise necessary caution but be reassured that this is not only a public bridleway but also crosses designated open country access land. Cross a boardwalk and follow blue markers around the marsh. Then walk beside a couple of old hedgebanks, still proceeding almost straight ahead, to leave the moor at a gate.

For the next 1,000 metres we follow a green lane through a lush landscape of ponds, scrub and woods to gradually climb out of the valley though a final gate beside delightful grounds at Springdale.

13 Follow its drive uphill and around to the right (SW),

beside Fairview, and continue straight ahead, passing the Old Forge, along the bank lane to the junction with Common Road and return to the western end of Smeatharpe hamlet in 500 metres.

Springdale.

8 Dunkeswell and Madford

A 6-mile circuit down the Madford River valley and back along quiet lanes

There are two Dunkeswell villages. The one with the visible mediaeval history is Dunkeswell Abbey. Dunkeswell itself, two miles down the valley of the Madford River, has St Nicholas parish church and the Royal Oak Inn, plus an historic heart, small-scale suburbia and large-scale light industry. Much has come about on land beside a wartime Coastal Command and United States Army Air Force base, which has evolved into a busy civilian airfield for light aircraft, helicopters, microlights and parachuting. There is also a gliding club which operates from a nearby

Level:

Length: 5.5 miles

Terrain: A comparatively easy progress down the valley with lanes for the return.

Park & start: In Dunkeswell Abbey hamlet which is two miles north of Dunkeswell village.

Start ref: ST 141 106

Postcode: EX14 0RP

Public transport: Buses between Honiton and Taunton (join the route at Dunkeswell village).

Websites:

www.maps.google.co.uk

www.wikipedia.org.uk/dunkeswell

airstrip. Both Dunkeswells and their linking lanes and paths are explored on this moderate-length walk.

Dunkeswell Abbey.

1. Set off along the path between Abbey View and Abbey Cottages. Explore the ruins of the Gatehouse and Abbot's Lodging and visit Holy Trinity Church. The onward path is through the churchyard, 100 metres from the gate, and across the wall under a yew tree in 20 metres.

2. Bear right (NE) in the field, following the stream to a bridge and gate. Cross the next

On 13 August 1201, Lord William de Briwere commissioned a dozen monks from Forde Abbey, with Brother Gregory as their foreman, to build the Abbey of Dunkeswell.

Picturesque ruins remain of Cistercian Dunkeswell Abbey which was largely demolished after the Dissolution of the Monasteries by Henry VIII in 1539.

meadow to the gates on the other side and then bridge the Madford River in 300 metres. Walk up to the gate to the right of the farmstead in 150 metres.

3. Turn left (N) and then right (E) at both junctions in 150 metres, beside thatched Prings Farm, uphill towards Upottery. Pass Madford Farm, Corunna and Way Close.

Madford River.

Abbot's coffin.

Prings farmhouse.

Old Park herd.

4 Turn right in 800 metres, at the summit, through Abbotsford Farm (S). Continue straight ahead into the pasture in 250 metres. Follow the top of the hillside and keep the hedge to the left for 200 metres. The path becomes a double-hedged green lane for 250 metres which we leave as it turns downhill. Fork left, over a stile, and now keep the hedge to your right.

Canadian émigré Elizabeth Posthuma Simcoe (1766-1850) and her daughters cherished their descent from William de Brewer and funded the building of Holy Trinity Church on the site of St Mary's Abbey Church in 1842.

(5) Turn to the right of a barn at Middle Mackham in 300 metres. Go down the steps and turn left. Fork right in 20 metres and also fork right below Higher Mackham Farm in 150 metres, into newly-created Somercombe Woof in 100 metres.

(6) Turn right (SW) in the second of these fields in 200 metres, down into the valley, to exit from the lower right-hand corner. Descend through a magical patch of ancient woodland and cross the river in 300 metres. Walk up through the remains of the farm at Old Park – destroyed by a Luftwaffe bomb in the Second World War – and continue straight ahead (S) in 300 metres. Bowerhayes Copse, down to the left, conceals eight lakes and ponds.

Dunkeswell lambs.

(7) Continue straight ahead from the parkland pasture, across a stile and then a gate in 200 metres, to cross a hillside pasture diagonally uphill to the gate in the far right-hand corner in 250 metres.

(8) Turn left, along a bridleway through Bowerhayes Farm, and then right (SW) in 100 metres. Cross a stile beneath a transformer pole just beyond the bungalow. Our route, which is unaffected by a nearby

bridge closure, follows the hedgerow along the top of the valley to Huntshayes Farm in 500 metres. Pass to the left of the buildings and follow the drive to the second corner in 300 metres.

(9) Turn left and follow the hedgerow with Dunkeswell Aerodrome across to the right. The bank and path follow the top of a precipitous wooded slope riddled with badger setts.

The fields of 35-acre Somercombe Wood, created as a carbon-offset project by co2balance.com are named Memorial Wood, Toshiba Wood and Mediacom Wood.

(10) Turn right (N) on reaching the road above Dunkeswell village in 400 metres (though you can continue for 500 metres to visit St Nicholas Church and the Royal Oak Inn). Proceed straight ahead at the junction at Bowerhayes Cross in 800 metres. Also continue along the road beside Higher Park Farm in a further 800 metres. The lane begins a steep descent from Higher Musgrove in another 800 metres. The final 800 metres, via Corner House and Abbey Cross Barn, end beside the Old School House at Dunkeswell Abbey.

Dunkeswell village.

Dunkeswell Aerodrome.

RAF Dunkeswell, constructed in 1943, hosted the 479th Antisubmarine Group of the United States Army Air Force, for operations against U-boats in the Bay of Biscay.

9 **Luppitt and Dumpdon**

A 9-mile round walk around deep-cut valley commons and pastures

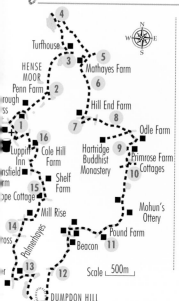

Level: 🥾 🥾 🥾
Length: 9 miles
Terrain: Hill country throughout with many of the tracks being across rugged landscape.
Park and start: In Luppitt by visiting St Mary's Church which has its car-park near the top of the hill.
Start ref: ST 169 068
Postcode: EX14 0RY
Public transport: None
Websites:
www.luppitt.net
www.white-hall-farm.co.uk

The hillsides and secret valleys of the Luppitt Commons comprise both the biggest site of special scientific interest and area of open country in the Blackdown Hills. Such land now enjoys a right of public access on foot for air and exercise. Parts are managed for hay-cuts, rough grazing and wildlife conservation but much remains impenetrably wild. The vegetation is generally bracken and gorse on the slopes, rowan and whitebeam on higher ground, and sallow scrub down in the valley bottoms. Stonechats and marsh fritillary butterflies are among the speciality species. Another wedge of common land, overlooking Honiton from Dumpdon Hill, is owned by the National Trust. An ancient country house, Mohun's Ottery with gateway carvings, preserves the name of the Barons Mohun.

(1) Set off uphill (NW) from Luppitt House to the triple junction at Ringborough Cross in 200 metres. Turn sharp right (NE) and pass Fairview Farm to the corner in 400 metres. Continue straight ahead along the track under power cables at the top of the valley. Pass Penn Farm in 200 metres and enter grassy access land where we join a public footpath and follow the upper hedgerow (N) in 300 metres.

Hartridge to Dumpdon.

Dumpdon Hill, a double-banked Iron Age fort dating from the 1st century BC, and 62 acres of common land were acquired by the National Trust in 1981.

Mathayes Farm.

2 This is Hense Moor, which is registered common land with a general right of public access on foot for air and exercise, so you can deviate from the official paths. Descend to cross the stream (NE) in the scrubby valley in 400 metres. Keep a smallholding and its clearing to your right as the public footpath crosses another gully and climbs to Turfhouse in 600 metres.

3 Turn left (N), beside the little woods, to continue up the main valley for 750 metres. The common becomes increasingly wooded.

4 Turn right (SE) up through the bracken and across the grassy slope as you approach the fields beyond the moor. Keep the common land boundary to your left for 600 metres. Join a farm track, from the fields, to cross the fence-line into scrubland along the top of the valley.

5 Turn right (SW) on reaching a farm road in 300 metres. Continue straight ahead through the gate into the hard-standing of Mathayes Farm in 50 metres. Turn left (S) in 100 metres, across a triangle of grass above the thatched farmhouse

Whitehall Farm's prized flock of curly-fleece Gotland sheep, descended from Viking stock on the Baltic island, graze the southern slopes of Dumpdon Hill.

and Otter Brewery depot. This skirts the garden and climbs to a gate at the top of the slope in 100 metres.

6 Cross the stile to the stile in the top left-hand corner of the pasture in 200 metres. Follow the hedgerow straight ahead and cross a stile at the end of the second hilltop pasture in 175 metres. Go through penning in the next area of grassland and walk the length of the final pasture. Join a track, downhill, beside sycamore and ash trees in 500 metres. Cross the stile and descend between the barns of Hill End Farm to turn left along its drive in 100 metres. Join a public road at the corner in 50 metres.

7 Proceed for 100 metres and turn left (E), up a stony green lane, to a tarred road in 250 metres.

8 Cross to the stony track on the other side. Although not a public road this can be used on foot as it crosses access land. Pass to the right of a barn in 200 metres. Descend to the road at a corner in 300 metres. Ignore the right-hand turning to Hartridge Buddhist Monastery and take the central option downhill (S) through Odle Farm in 200 metres.

Off roading.

9 Continue straight ahead beside Primrose Farm Cottages after which the road becomes a grassy lane. In 500 metres this goes through a gate and passes a small wood to a multiple junction in 100 metres.

Hill End Farm.

Wayside bull.

10 Find signs for the bridleway. This is the lesser path – the second track to the left – into the arable field towards the masts above Honiton. Follow the dense hedgerow which you keep to your right with the valley (and sound of A30 traffic) across to the left. Pass a wood to the left in 500 metres and a barn to the right in a further 200 metres. The bridleway becomes a wide green lane and passes Mohun's Ottery in 400 metres. Join its drive, to a road junction at Pound Farm, in 600 metres.

11 Turn right (NW) uphill into Beacon hamlet in 500 metres. Turn left (S) at the first junction. Continue straight ahead at the second in 100 metres. Bear left at the third in 50 metres.

12 Continue to Dumpdon Hill in 750 metres. Turn right and then left at the corner to climb across National Trust land to the Iron Age fort on the summit in 500 metres. Turn right (W) and descend to a track on the wilder slopes overlooking Honiton.

Hawkridge.

Turn right (N) and return to the road in 500 metres.

Links between Mohun's Ottery and its founding family include John Meade Falkner's Victorian smuggling adventure Moonfleet *and the place-name Hammoon in Dorset's Blackmore Vale.*

Mohun's Ottery.

13 Turn left (SW) down to Palmerhayes and the junction at Wick Cross in 500 metres. Turn right (N) beside Higher Wick Farm, and pass Rolleshayes Farm. Continue straight ahead at Barn Cross in 900 metres. Proceed to the next cross-roads at Mill Rise in 300 metres.

14 Turn right (E), into a cul-de-sac, and then straight ahead into a narrow, stony green lane. This climbs to Shelves Farm in 750 metres and the road on a corner beside thatched Antelope Cottage.

15 Turn left (N), downhill, to pass Shelf Farm to the junction beside Barnfield Farm in 750 metres. Turn right here. Also turn right between the cottage and the bridge in 200 metres. The path into the pastures follows the stream to a footbridge and lane in 250 metres.

16 Turn left (E), to the corner in 150 metres, and right (N) at Cole Hill Farm. The bridleway bears left beside Brook Cottage outbuilding – uphill across common land – to a road in 400 metres. Turn left (SW) to Luppitt Inn in 300 metres. Turn right (N) to return to the parish church in 150 metres.

Luppitt cottage.

Beacon hamlet.

10 Cotleigh and Stockland Hill

A 7.5-mile circuit of the lush lands beneath Stockland Hill television transmitter

Flat-topped hills, with a couple of early Iron Age hill-forts in the vicinity, are separated by the valley of the Umborne Brook. The river is crossed four times in the course of this walk. We also follow the equally scenic Corry Brook and its mill-leat through Millhayes. The largely pastoral landscape is well-wooded.

Highland cattle at Royal Oak Farm add to the character. Cottages tend to cluster around mills rather than churches – at both Cotleigh and Millhayes – which shows how settlement patterns have been driven by natural resources. Many of the place-names indicate that the enclosures or 'hayes' have been cleared from primeval woodland in historic times.

Level: 🥾 🥾
Length: 7.5 miles
Terrain: Ups and downs of valley walking, often along stony tracks, though without steep slopes.
Park & start: From St Michael's Church at Cotleigh.
Start ref: ST 206 022
Postcode: EX14 9HF
Public transport: None
Websites:
www.ukvillages.co.uk/cotleigh
www.villages.co.uk

Map labels:
Featherlake
Lower Brimpit Farm
WOOD COPSE
Post Lane
Neroche
Langbeer Farm
South Wood Farm
Umborne Brook
Hornshayes
Corry Brook
Stockland Little Castle
Millhayes
Bull Farm
Cotleigh Bridge
Royal Oak Farm
Newlands
...eigh ...en Lane
Wellhayes Farm
Cotleigh Mill
Cotleigh
Pidgeon's Cottage
Scale 500m

5 6 4 7 8 3 12 11 10 9 13 2 14 1 15

Cotleigh and Stockland Hill

1 Set off along the church path (N), beside the tower, and join Gully Lane on the other side of the church-yard. This becomes a green lane and crosses a stream above a ravine. Follow the track uphill to a road in 500 metres.

2 Turn left to the junction at Holmleigh Green, in 100 metres. Pass Antlers on the right, in 75 metres, and then turn left in 15 metres, through the field gate. Walk straight ahead down to the gate in the hedge between the thatched cottages in 200 metres. Bear right in the pasture, up to the gate on the far side in 200 metres. Turn left across the field, along the top of the slope, to bushes between Bull Farm and the cottage in 300 metres. Turn right, through the gates, to the road above Oak Cottage in 50 metres.

Cotleigh Church.

Holmsleigh oak.

Wood Copse ferns.

Fifteenth-century Sir Ralph le Jewe – a martyred Christian convert – is commemorated by a sword in the shape of a cross beside the contemporary Beerstone font in Cotleigh Church.

3 Turn left (NE) at the road junction in 20 metres. Follow this lane for 150 metres. Turn left (N)

between the oak trees at the top of the slope, through the field gate, and follow hedgerows straight ahead to South Wood Farm in 700 metres. Turn left up its drive, to the road in 75 metres.

4 Turn right (NE), along what becomes a green lane beside North Wood Cottage, after the second corner in 250 metres. Bear right in Wood Copse, following the bridleway, downhill across Umborne Brook at the footbridge and ford. Climb up the

cherty hollow way, out of the wood and across fields, to the house and road in 800 metres.

5 Turn right (E), to pass Neroche, up Post Lane to the road junction in 600 metres.

6 Turn left and then right, through the field gate, in 75 metres. Follow the hedgerow ahead to the next gate in 150 metres. Bear right (SE) down to the wood below the hillside pasture. Follow the track to the right of Featherlake and down its drive, passing Lower Brimpit Farm to the road in 800 metres.

Cotleigh takes its name from 'Cotta's-leah' (Cotta's meadow).

Umborne Brook.

Farms and cottages in this part of Devon were without mains electricity until the 160-feet pylons of the national grid were constructed along the South Coast from Dungeness in 1958.

Lower Brimpit Farm.

7 Turn right (S) to the junction in 100 metres. Turn left (E), down the lane beside Langbeer Farm, to the next junction after Hornhayes in 800 metres.

8 Cross to the drive (S) beside the sign and go over a stile into the field. Follow the hedge and Corry Brook to the corner of the field and cross a footbridge there, in 200 metres. Turn right, up the slope for 20 metres, and turn left beside the sign for Huntshayes Farm. Follow the mill leat to Millhayes Cottage in 300 metres. The pit for the mill-wheel is beside its wall.

9 Turn right up the lane and fork left on the hillside in 200 metres. Turn left and then right (SW) at the junction, beside Chapel Croft in 50 metres, up Hussey's Lane towards Shore Bottom.

10 Turn right (N) on reaching Newlands in 250 metres. Follow the green lane to the left-hand gate in 250 metres. Follow the hedge (SW) up to the wood which you keep to your left. The television transmitter is across to the left and the earthworks of Stockland Little Castle down to the right. Proceed to the top left-hand side of the pasture in 300 metres.

Highland cattle.

11 Cross Shrubbery Lane to the left-hand gate on the other side. Follow the hedgerow (W) to the right-hand end of the skyline trees, to a gate on to the road in 600 metres.

12 Turn left and go straight ahead at the cross-roads in 100 metres. Follow the Old Chard Road downhill. Pass the lawn cafe at Royal Oak Farm in 300 metres. Thatched Little Snodwell is next and the road re-

crosses the brook at Cotleigh Bridge in 600 metres. Pass Brookside Lodge, uphill for 250 metres, and turn left through the gate opposite the farm entrance.

13 Bear right (SW) across the field, to the right of Wellhayes Farm, in 200 metres. Continue straight ahead – through the field gate – and follow the hedgerow down to a stile and along a track from the farmyard to a green lane in 250 metres.

The great landmark of these parts, erected in 1960, is the 750-feet television transmitter which stands on the 775-feet contour at Stockland Hill.

Stockland Hill Transmitter.

Little Snodwell.

(14) Turn left, over the culvert, and up a hollow way, to a junction of tracks in 200 metres. Turn left (SE), passing Monday Cottage, and cross the brook for the third time after Cotleigh Mill in 300 metres. Follow the path uphill, across a stile in 125 metres, and another in a further 125 metres. Bear left on the other side of the hedge, up to the far corner of the freshly wooded pasture in 300 metres. Turn right (S), and keeping the older wood to your left, and enter the next field through a gate in 75 metres. Follow the hedgerow straight ahead, with Stockland Hill

The circular earthwork of Stockland Little Castle was a palisaded bank around an Iron Age settlement.

transmitter up to the left, in this field and the next to the road in 500 metres.

(15) Turn right (W), downhill, and follow it back across the brook, upstream from Pidgeon's Cottage, in 300 metres. Follow the road uphill to the Old Rectory and the church in 600 metres.

Corry Brook.

Stockland Little Castle.

FLOWERS of the CHINESE CALENDAR

January	Plum Blossom
February	Peach Blossom
March	Tree Peony
April	Cherry Blossom
May	Magnolia
June	Pomegranate
July	Lotus
August	Pear Blossom
September	Mallow
October	Chrysanthemum
November	Gardenia
December	Poppy

FLOWERS of the JAPANESE CALENDAR

January	Pine
February	Plum
March	Peach, Pear
April	Cherry
May	Azalea, Peony, Wisteria
June	Iris
July	Morning Glory
August	Lotus
September	Autumn's Seven Grasses
October	Chrysanthemum
November	Maple
December	Camellia

THE PREPARATION and CARE of CUT FLOWERS

If you put the following techniques into practice you will extend the life of your flowers by at least a week. The science behind it is rather dull but the results are amazing!

When picking flowers do it as early in the day as possible and choose ones that are already half open. Immediately after picking or receiving your flowers remove any damaged or wilted leaves and re-cut the stems about an inch from the base making sure you cut on the diagonal. The ends of woody stems should be split by several inches with scissors or a sharp knife. Any stems which exude a milky sap should have their cut ends seared in candle flame for a few seconds. Knobbly-stemmed flowers like pinks and carnations should be cut just above a node, not immediately below. Only the green part of fleshy-stemmed flowers like hyacinths, gladioli and irises is able to absorb water, so make sure you cut off their white base. After this preparation, plunge the flowers up to their necks in a bucket of tepid water and leave them to soak for several hours before arranging them.